OVERCOMING:

A Survival Guide for Change Agents

OVERCOMING:

A Survival Guide for Change Agents

GREG WALLACE

The Wallace Group
2015

Graphics by Gustavo Jimenez | Spotmill

Unless otherwise identified, Scripture quotations are taken from the New King James Version. Copyright © 1982 by Thomas Nelson, Inc. Used by permission. All rights reserved. Scripture quotations marked NLT are taken from the Holy Bible, New Living Translation, copyright 1996, 2004. Used by permission of Tyndale House Publishers., Wheaton, Illinois 60189. All rights reserved. All emphasis is the author's own.

ISBN 978-0-9964493-1-1

Table of Contents

PROLOGUE

And so it was that the chief executive officer (CEO) and his leadership team had reached an impasse. The progress of their organization had come to a grinding halt.

After much previous success, this was a surprising development. The CEO was tall in stature and widely known. Both literally and figuratively he was head and shoulders above his competition for the top job.

In the early years of his tenure he had built a solid leadership team, repelled several hostile takeover attempts, and devised strategies that demolished competitors in his company's market. Now faced with a huge obstacle that prevented any further advance, the CEO and his leadership team needed a way out of the quandary.

The CEO offered a significant performance bonus to incentivize his leaders to act, but to no avail. Day after day his organization languished in the slow death of inaction. Even more disheartening to the CEO was the realization that none of his handpicked leaders had a clue how to answer the threat to the firm's well-being. He knew that unless an answer was forthcoming, it would be lights out for the company.

One day a former employee of the CEO came back on staff. He was experienced in overcoming difficult circumstances and announced that he had a change plan that would rescue the organization.

Despite the perilous circumstances the CEO and his leaders faced, the change agent's announcement was not well-received. The leadership team had no faith in him. The CEO's commitment to his offer was shaky. The intended beneficiaries of the change did not actively support him or his ideas.

Besides the difficulties inherent in implementing change, the change agent faced fierce resistance from within the ranks. He knew that unless he managed it well, this so-called *friendly fire* could derail any and all progress.

Yet, the change agent was confident that his skills and experience were right for the job. He took on the external challenge and those within the organization. He operated outside the culture and rejected old ways of working. Unlike the organization's leaders, he expanded his focus. He not only understood which changes were needed; he knew *why* they were needed.

Through a combination of boldness and courage, he produced a victory. Friendly fire was overcome, the biggest obstacles to change were vanquished, the organization prevailed over its competitor's threat, and the CEO reached his goals.

The change was not easy; but it was worth it.

PART I
CHANGE
ESSENTIALS

CHAPTER ONE

THE OLD IS NOW, AGAIN

It's axiomatic that the only constant in the corporate world is change. The axiom is not new; it has played out for centuries.

The prologue you just read describes the long-ago battle in which a young man named David rescued King Saul and the army of Israel from the threat of Goliath, the Philistine army's larger-than-life champion. The incident occurred hundreds of years before we started using A.D. to designate calendar years. Yet it is a timely example of a leader willing to change the normal ways of conducting business in order to overcome challenges to an organization's survival.

In the Old Testament account, the army of Israel was stymied by the Philistines—in particular, by the giant named Goliath.[1] King Saul was "dismayed" by the stalemate. The soldiers in his army were

---

[1] See the Bible's Book of First Samuel, chapter 17.

dismayed, too. They fled before the presence and reputation of Goliath.

Defeat seemed inevitable when David arrived upon the scene unannounced. He was there to run an errand for his father and wondered why everyone was so afraid of one man. He perceived an opportunity for victory and offered to take on the Philistine warrior.

The leaders of Saul's army scoffed. Even the king declared that David was just a boy who had no chance of winning. But David insisted and the king relented. Saul agreed to send him into battle and tried to give David his own armor and weapons to use. David rejected them.

> "Giants are not what we think they are. The same qualities that appear to give them strength are often the sources of great weakness."
> — Malcolm Gladwell, *David and Goliath*

When David finally stepped onto the battlefield to face Goliath—all nine feet, six inches of him—he did it alone. Not one soldier was willing to accompany him. Yet David remained confident. His memories of previous victories over a lion and a bear were fresh in his mind, and he was motivated by the righteousness of the cause. David's self-assurance, sense of purpose, and skillful use of his chosen weapons allowed him to do what seemed impossible.

David slew Goliath, and Israel's army prevailed.

Theme for the Ages

The underdog-overcoming-impossible-odds theme is so iconic that it is universal. *Whenever a person, team, or organization faces a seemingly overwhelming challenge, we invoke the metaphor of David and Goliath.* And when the underdog triumphs, we simply say, "David has defeated Goliath!"

A Google search of David and Goliath images yields illustrations of the ancient battle and contemporary images that evoke the metaphor: a photo of a small child facing off against a sumo wrestler; a man throwing a rock at an armored tank; pictures of the compact but mighty martial artist Bruce Lee standing up to Kareem Abdul-Jabbar, the seven-foot-two-inch basketball legend.

These images point to what many change agents (consultants, HR professionals, and others who have been tasked to implement change in an organization) know all too well: overcoming the challenge of change is hard.

No wonder so many books have been written about it.

YOUR SIDE OF THE METAPHOR

Being "a David" is part of the change agent's job description. The underdog role results from having a vision the giant cannot yet see. If it is communicated, your vision is powerful enough to confront the towering status quo and soften the resistance. The fear of change is dissolved in the white-hot atmosphere of innovation.

Survival Tip for Assessing the Cause: *Remember That Victors Are Human*

We can read David's writings, but if we could talk with him over latte, we might be tempted to ask the victory questions: "How did you develop your stone-and-sling strategy? How did your self-talk sound as you ran toward Goliath?[2] Did the Israelite soldiers change their tune once you killed him?"

If I were sitting with David, I would remind myself to probe the tough-as-nails side of his story—the taunts of his oldest brother, Eliab; the skepticism of the king; the inglorious history of Goliath's manipulation of Israel's army; the dangerous and unbalanced equation of "boy versus seasoned warrior."

David's inner and outer struggles were as much a part of his victory as his audacious courage was. Recognizing the humanity of successful change agents is as important as modeling their victories. Find mentors who are willing to share the unglamorous details of their storied journeys. Let their human frailties remind you that successful change agents are ordinary people who are extraordinarily committed to the mission of transformation.

---

[2] David's chosen weapons were five stones and a sling designed to launch them. He used only one of the stones and did indeed run toward his enemy. The details are found in the Book of First Samuel, chapter 17.

Sparking the Change

1. Describe a stalemate at your firm, ministry, or organization that prompts you to become part of the solution. How did the stagnancy develop, in your opinion? Who else is aware of the need for change and willing to talk about it?

2. Is there a "David and Goliath" aspect to the situation you just described? Who plays the role of David? Goliath? King Saul? Israel's army? How might the ancient story inform your approach to the task at hand?

3. How do you feel empowered as a change agent in this situation? Is your confidence based in the facts, or are you confident in spite of them? Which circumstances or people seem to be the most intimidating? Is your assessment based in the reality on the ground or your perception of it (*i.e.,* your own doubts that change is possible)?

CHAPTER TWO

CHANGE AGENTS, THIS ONE'S FOR YOU

Since its publication in 1998, Dr. Spencer Johnson's bestseller, *Who Moved My Cheese?*, has come to represent the inevitability and pervasiveness of change. Numerous books have since been written to guide leaders as they spearhead change. Other books help employees adapt to it. And still others help change agents with the nuts and bolts of implementation.

However, few books have been written specifically for change agents with the goal of helping them survive the rigors of leading long-term organizational culture change.

That is the goal of *this* book.

Changes in organizational culture are particularly daunting. "Because it is durable and resistant to major change, corporate culture requires the investment of a great deal of time and resources before it can be modified."[3]

Culture can be described as a group's shared values, attitudes, and beliefs. Changes to culture are necessary when leaders recognize that those values, attitudes, and beliefs are misaligned with the goals and strategies ahead.

For the purposes of this book, organizational culture change is what modifies a group's shared values, attitudes, and beliefs. It does not refer to change initiatives that accompany, for instance, the implementation of a new technology within a work group. Those initiatives tend to be shorter and more targeted. Neither does organizational culture change refer to initiatives that develop a change-resilient culture, such as providing employees with training, tools, and techniques to cope

> "The marathon can...expose all your nerve endings and bring you closer to recognizing the real you, all flaws and virtues on the surface."
> — Hal Higdon, Marathon: The Ultimate Training Guide

---

[3] Daryl R. Connor, *Managing at the Speed of Change* (New York: Random House, 1993), 179.

more effectively with an environment that is frequently in flux.

Organizational culture change is the *Goliath of change.*

Imagine running a 26.2-mile marathon. The distance alone is challenging. Now imagine running a 26.2 mile obstacle course full of hurdles, rugged terrain, swamps, and rivers. Further imagine that this course is not only uncharted, but ever-changing. Just when you think you have it figured out, it morphs into something else.

This is a fair description of what it takes and how it feels to change an organization's culture. It is a long, difficult, and unpredictable journey. And "if your organization's current culture and the change you want to make in the company have little in common, your chances of successfully achieving that change are slim."[4]

Because of the difficulty, this type of change takes time. Most experts estimate that a minimum of three

---

[4] Daryl R. Connor, *Managing at the Speed of Change* (New York: Random House, 2006), 178.

years and as many as seven years are needed to complete an organizational culture change.

Change agents therefore face the daunting task of remaining on point for a battle that is both long and exceedingly difficult to win. They will face resisters and create enemies. They are likely to cross swords with their bosses, and they run the risk of burning themselves out before the battle is over.

Thus, many change efforts fail long before they reach the finish line. The commitment to be counted among the "slim" number of success stories can weigh heavily upon and even wear out the change agent.

I should know.[5]

One of my change assignments was in support of a senior leader's desire to improve the culture of her organization. The change initiative was designed, among other things, to improve the way employees related to one another.

After two years, there were some successes, but much work still needed to be done. It was clear that the workplace was filled with people deeply wounded by past and present leaders. Middle managers who had been hurt wore their feelings on their sleeves. They were, in fact, infecting others with their negativity and lack of self-esteem.

In those two years, I had earned the trust of most of the employees. This afforded me a certain amount of influence. It meant that I was a safe place for people to vent their frustrations, hurts, and complaints.

Being that safe place has its price. One day, within five minutes of walking into the building, I found myself on the other end of someone's complaint. More than that, I became the stand-in for the person they were complaining about. *Bam!* I received the brunt of someone's dissatisfaction.

Fewer than five minutes after our one-way conversation, I was on the receiving end of someone else's anger and frustration. Again, I stood in for the person who had generated these intense feelings, and I absorbed the offended party's fury.

---

[5] In order to be constructively candid about my experiences, I have placed some of the anecdotes in a different context to protect the innocent, the guilty (and me!).

This was not unusual for me. Even having such intense conversations compacted in a short time frame was routine. But this day, for whatever reason, was different. As I turned from the second encounter and headed to my office, I started to cry. By the time I reached my desk I was bawling like a baby. I don't know exactly how long I wept, but it was a good while before I stopped.

Here I was, an experienced leader, a capable manager, a veteran change agent, and back-to-back encounters reduced me to tears. I realized that these two conversations had not brought me to this place. It was not even the week or month of drama-filled exchanges; it was the cumulative effect of trying to implement change in a change-resistant environment.

This double-barreled episode illustrates the reality that change is hard and changing the culture of an organization is *extremely* hard. It also highlights why change agents are the primary audience for this book. Every day, they face their giants with nothing but a slingshot and five smooth stones.

My fellow change agent, there are Davids like you everywhere! They overcome the difficulties and bring organizations into their desired state. May you find in the pages ahead the wherewithal to thrive until *you* can enjoy the benefits of the change you helped to create.

> **RUNNING THE RACE**
>
> David enjoyed the fruits of his labor, but his success did not come overnight. David ran a long, arduous race marked by sweet victories and bitter losses. He was familiar with the highs and lows of change-making. He celebrated and shed his share of tears. The thread running through it all was David's willingness to weather the ups and downs and finish the course. David took some lumps, but he left a legacy.

Survival Tip for Staying in the "Race": *Stay Humble*

Renowned running expert Hal Higdon warns that "running 26.2 miles...can be a humbling experience."[6] Runners have to accept the race as it is. A dry course, moderate temperatures, and low humidity might be ideal, but weather does not always cooperate with runners' wishes. They must run the course as they find it, and that can be humbling.

---

[6] Hal Higdon, *Marathon: The Ultimate Training Guide* (New York: Rodale Books, 2011).

As a change agent you must also deal with circumstances as they are. You are recruited because the cultural environment is challenging. Resistance is inevitable. The other "runners" have their own ideas about what the finish line should look like. Competition can be fierce and chaotic, yet you are charged with herding the entrants toward a common goal, even when the rigors of the course challenge your mind and body.

A key ingredient to staying in the race is to stay humble. Don't take the resistance personally. When an angry, frustrated staffer uses you as a stand-in, remind yourself that it really isn't about you. You are there as a bridge to change, so everybody can win.

Sparking the Change

1. It is no small task to "move someone else's cheese"—no less *everybody's* cheese in an organization. Describe your sense of legitimacy (or lack thereof) in performing this task. What light does your answer shed on your past and current performance?

2. How realistic are your expectations in terms of the time it takes to facilitate an organization's cultural change? To what, if any, degree does your answer reveal a desire to "shorten the race" and limit the pain involved in running it?

3. Describe your most memorable or most recent meltdown as a change agent. What event(s) triggered your reaction? What was the deeper cause?

CHAPTER THREE

THE UNIVERSAL CHALLENGE OF CHANGE

As we examine the work of change, we will see why it is so difficult and why strong men and women are sometimes tempted to walk away from it. One obvious reason is that organizational change threatens the security of leaders, employees, and the organization itself. When that happens, past successes can be among the highest hurdles to clear.

One change I was asked to lead involved transforming a culture that valued individual and group success into one in which team and organizational success were valued. The leaders of several operational departments were highly tenured and highly regarded. As a result, they were highly compensated. Now their departments were merged to create a single division under a newly appointed vice president hired from outside the company.

The vice president led the new division as a collection of distinct departments rather than one organization. No doubt the power, influence, and successful track records of his direct reports influenced his management choices. He lasted less than eighteen months.

His successor understood that this reconfigured unit would not succeed if unaligned departments continued to pursue their individual visions, missions, and strategies. He issued what seemed to be a simple request to the department heads: *Work as a team.* Because the department heads liked and respected each other, the V.P. expected the mandate would be easily fulfilled.

"Not so fast!" says the voice of hindsight.

To department leaders who had achieved success as individual contributors, the change was perceived as a threat. They were being asked to work differently. It meant putting the interests of the division ahead of the interests of their departments. They had worked hard to master their ways of succeeding. As they saw it, their unfortunate reward was to now surrender their credentials as experienced individual contributors and become apprentice-level team players. Their success (and their raises) had once been as certain as their biweekly paychecks. Now success (and their raises) became uncertain.

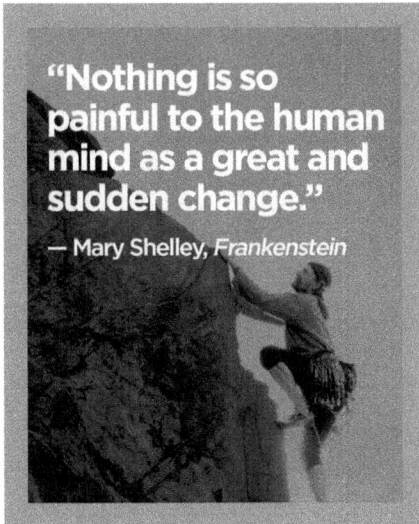

> "Nothing is so painful to the human mind as a great and sudden change."
> — Mary Shelley, *Frankenstein*

Needless to say, these leaders were not the most enthusiastic supporters of the change.

Even though working with colleagues was not a particularly onerous prospect, change meant doing it in unfamiliar ways, with untested implications. Suddenly, working as a team meant their peers could influence how their work was done and the results they produced.

Because of this threat to individual success, change agents often embark on the difficult task of managing an organizational culture change initiative with little support.

This is the underexplored bane of the change agent! Understanding the reason for the change and creating a clear vision for change are essential. So is the building of guiding coalitions. But navigating the process with little support is central to the change agent's arduous journey.

The detailed process of change is covered extensively by many excellent authors. We are more focused on the change agents than the process. Our assumption is that David has the strategy, skill, experience, and knowledge to defeat Goliath. The question is: Can he survive the battle?

THE REAL POINT

David's skill in slaying Goliath with a pebble shot from a sling was impressive, but we are not here to discuss new approaches to giant-killing. Our focus is you, the change agent. When you are tempted to throw in the towel, knowing why you feel that way can be the key to overcoming.

Survival Tip for Overcoming Challenges: *Recognize Them*

You have heard the term *fog of war.* It is the "...uncertainty in situational awareness experienced by participants in military operations..."[7] In the midst of battle, it can be difficult to accurately perceive events and experiences, but easy to react to them. For this reason, the battle is often lost in the fog of war.

Change agents don't face the life-threatening challenges military personnel face on the battlefield. Yet a similar fog can affect their perceptions. Two simple tactics can cut through it: One is to glean from the experiences of other change agents. Hearing someone else's story can shed light on yours. The second is to look at the bigger picture. Take the example of the division vice president you just read about. He understood a great deal about the change process. He knew his team had to coalesce around a unified objective, and he accurately assessed his team members' regard for one another. Had he taken a slightly more panoramic view, he might have anticipated their fears.

When the fog of war rolls in, glean from others and think "big picture."

Sparking the Change

1. Do you suspect that prior successes have become obstacles on the path to organizational culture change? How does knowing this empower you to mitigate the challenges?

2. How might the fear of failing as a change agent make dealing with the fears of other stakeholders more complicated?

3. Assess your level of situational awareness. Which issues are you most clear about? Which are or were caught in a blind spot?

---

[7] *Wikipedia,* s.v. "the fog of war," http://www.en.wikipedia.org/wiki/Fog_of_war (accessed August 15, 2014).

CHAPTER FOUR

WHAT FRIENDLY FIRE LOOKS LIKE

One of the primary reasons the Goliath of change is so difficult on change agents is the friendly fire they must endure. Change is tough to implement under the best circumstances. "When there is major change there is resistance."[8] Even when the change agent has positional authority to direct the beneficiaries of change, and even when there is strong and committed leadership, change is hard. The reason is simple: "organization and change are not complementary concepts."[9]

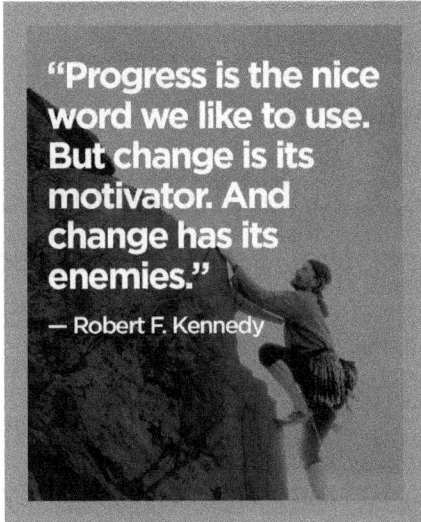

> "Progress is the nice word we like to use. But change is its motivator. And change has its enemies."
>
> — Robert F. Kennedy

---

[8] Daryl R. Connor, *Managing at the Speed of Change* (New York: Random House, 1993), 129.
[9] Robert E. Quinn, *Deep Change: Discovering the Leader Within* (San Francisco: Jossey-Bass, 1996), 5.

The Friendly Fire "4-1-1"

When the task of facilitating change is given to someone other than the senior leader, *the change agent faces a set of tough challenges that I call "friendly fire." These are internally driven challenges that impact the change agent and the change initiative.* Friendly fire comes in many forms. We will preview them here and delve deeper in coming chapters. As you read, ask yourself which scenarios help to explain the difficulties you face.

Lack of Positional Authority

Change agents appointed by top executives to lead change efforts usually lack the positional power necessary to drive change. This is because "they don't function as decision makers regarding change."[10] Under these conditions change agents rely on their ability to influence leaders to act differently. They cannot *direct* them to act differently.

In most movies about a teacher trying to win over doubting students, the teacher's influence rests upon the ability to win over the student who is most

---

[10] Daryl R. Connor, *Managing at the Speed of Change* (New York: Random House, 1993), 152.

respected, feared, or admired by other students. In such scenarios, the teacher might have positional authority. But as long as the student has greater influence, the teacher's positional authority is compromised.

Change agents must learn to influence people with or without the benefit of positional authority.

Lack of Strong Leadership Commitment

The heads of organizations who launch change initiatives generally support those initiatives. Their management teams might not be as keen, however. *The lack of support from high level leaders is a significant hurdle that must be overcome if the change agent is to be successful.*

Imagine a volleyball team that is playing well and has developed into a close-knit group. Although they have achieved great success, the coach wants them to learn a different style of play. So he brings in a new player to help facilitate the new style.

As you can imagine, the reception given to the new player might be less than warm. As the change agent, the new player needs the commitment of the leadership team. Presumably, he has the coach's support. Nevertheless, he will have to win the support of team leaders whose past success and comfortable chemistry could make his task difficult.

Lack of Enthusiastic Support from the Frontlines

One of my earliest lessons related to the implementation of change occurred when I managed a work group. The experience was a lesson in human nature. I was attempting to give group members more autonomy and greater decision-making authority. However, they continued to ask me to confirm major decisions.

When I expressed my frustration to a consultant, she offered an analogy comparing the members of the group to lions raised in confined environments. When such lions are given the opportunity to run free in the wild, they hesitate. It takes time for their behavior to adapt to their changed realities. The consultant believed that this highly tenured work group was slow to recognize that they were now operating in a different environment and needed more time to adapt.

Change agents may need to forego active and visible support from the beneficiaries of change until those beneficiaries adapt their behavior to their changed realities.

Loss of Clarity in Regard to the Change Vision

What happens when the senior leader no longer visibly supports the change vision? Even if the lack of support does not doom the initiative, it will certainly hamper its completion. Sometimes, the support of others in the organization continues despite the withdrawal of support from the top. Amazingly, the change initiative can maintain some momentum.

We will examine such scenarios more closely later. For now, it is important to know that *even with a loss of support from the senior leadership (a common development), the change agent can succeed.* The key is to get the work group to behave like a basketball team whose coach has been ejected from the game. The change agent's job is to keep the squad on the court. As long as they continue to play, the mission can be accomplished.

Misunderstanding Ownership

Another kind of trap lies in wait for change agents. Those who have a strong belief in the change vision and are credible enough to exercise significant influence are particularly susceptible because this trap is not set by others. Change agents lay this one for themselves.

I am reminded of a scene from the movie, *Dave.* The owner of a temp agency has been hired to impersonate the President of the United States. His only job is to wave to the crowd as he makes his way from a hotel to the presidential limousine. It is not a speaking part and nothing else is required of him.

But, emboldened by the cheering crowd, he blurts out, "Hello America! God bless you!"[11] A secret service agent is clearly not amused and yanks Dave into the limo. The imposter says sheepishly, "Sorry, I couldn't help it. I just got carried away."[12]

What change agent doesn't dream of taking the lead role and owning the change? Sometimes they do

---

[11] Dave, released by Warner Bros., 1993, screenplay by Gary Ross. See IMDb, "Dave," http://www.imdb.com/title/tt0106673/) and "Dave," Screenplays for You, http://sfy.ru/?script=dave (accessed August 23, 2014).

it unintentionally. Like the president's impersonator, they get carried away by a little success. In *Dave,* the mastermind of the impersonation plot became fed up with Dave's misunderstanding of ownership, and said what many organization leaders are tempted to say: "It's not his job—it's my job!"[13]

Therein lays the trap. *Change agents—especially strong ones—must avoid delusions about who they are. They are responsible for facilitating the change, but they don't "own" it.* They can mistakenly believe that they have ultimate decision-making power over the mission when they don't. That is the purview of the organization's leader, who might be tempted to say, "Don't pay any attention to him. He thinks *he's* the boss!"

CHANGE AGENT, KNOW THYSELF

David dealt with all kinds of friendly fire before going against Goliath. He was ridiculed by his brother and reminded of his shortcomings by the king. Yet he did a great job of gaining the king's support, albeit temporary, and sticking to his assignment as change agent. David killed the giant, forcing the king's army (including his own siblings) to accept a new reality; but even after his victory, David never deluded himself into believing he had the authority to act as king.

---

[12] Ibid.
[13] Ibid.

Survival Tip for Overcoming Friendly Fire: *Correctly Assess the Source*

As Robert Kennedy said, "Change has its enemies."[14] This is the reality you, the change agent, must accept. That being said, it is important to understand which "enemy" is producing the friendly fire you face.

The "enemy" is not a person, even though certain people seem to oppose the change you are initiating. Many forms of friendly fire are inherent in human nature and in organizational change. Some is rooted in misunderstanding or misplaced fear. Some is part of the growth process, as in the case of the work group that insisted on my confirming the decisions I empowered them to make.

Remember that the resistance is rarely personal. Your job is to discover...

> 1. How to succeed despite your lack of positional authority

---

[14] Robert F. Kennedy, "Address before the United States Congress of Mayors," May 25, 1964, the Department of Justice Library,

2. Whether you have the strong commitment of the leadership

3. The real reason those on the frontlines seem unenthusiastic

4. Whether and why the senior leader's vision is losing clarity

5. Whether you are misreading your role

Friendly fire need not be deadly to your cause. It can be a fantastic opportunity to make creative adjustments.

Sparking the Change

1. Even friendly fire stings. How have you reacted to it in the past? How might your approach be more productive in the future?

2. What friendly fire have you faced from senior and other leadership? Is there a pattern? What can you learn from it?

---

http://www.justice.gov/ag/rfkspeeches/1964/05-25-1964.pdf (accessed August 15, 2014).

3. Have you operated under any misunderstanding of your role, especially in regard to positional authority? How did it affect your relationship with leaders and with those on the frontlines?

PART II
SOURCES OF
FRIENDLY FIRE

CHAPTER FIVE

LACK OF POSITIONAL AUTHORITY

During a particular change initiative, I felt like David, a shepherd in the midst of warriors. I had no armor or high-powered weapons and I lacked the power to issue orders. Yet I was tasked to change the behavior of the soldiers. Even when it was unspoken, I faced the kind of cynicism David's brother dished out:

> Now Eliab his oldest brother heard when he spoke to the men; and Eliab's anger was aroused against David, and he said, "Why did you come down here? And with whom have you left those few sheep in the wilderness? I know your pride and the insolence of your heart, for you have come down to see the battle" (1 Samuel 17:28).

Eliab was dismissive of his younger brother. "Aren't you just a shepherd boy? Aren't you just here to see what the real men are doing?"

Have you ever launched a change initiative that did not include some Eliabs? I doubt it. They are part of the change landscape for many of the reasons we have already discussed. They are stakeholders in the organization's status quo and change threatens their stakes.

The change agent, on the other hand, is invested in the mandated new direction. Here is the catch: *although change agents are held at least partly responsible for making change happen, they don't always possess the same power and authority as other leaders.*

This was the challenge I faced in an assignment mentioned in a previous chapter. The senior vice president formed a new division comprised of four previously separate organizations, and he hired a new vice president to lead it. The division employed over two thousand people and had a $200 million budget. Each of the four departments was led by an experienced director. Three of the directors had worked for the company for more than twenty years, and all four were very successful. They also enjoyed reporting directly to the senior V.P. Now, they saw reporting to a "mere" vice president as a demotion.

This put the vice president in an extremely difficult position. He was not familiar with the culture, the players, and the history of the organization. More importantly, he was in a hurry and employed few organizational change techniques. Ironically, one of his direct reports was in the thick of her own department's organizational change effort. It did not reinforce the larger mandate; it reinforced the walls of her well-siloed department.

> "Change is hard because people overestimate the value of what they have—and underestimate the value of what they may gain by giving that up."
>
> — James Belasco and Ralph Stayer, *Flight of the Buffalo*

A Division Divided

The new division vice president lasted less than eighteen months. He was unable to improve the division's performance, partly because the directors continued to work as individuals rather than as a team. All four units maintained unique vision statements, mission statements, strategic plans—you get the idea. The division had no unifying...well, no unifying *anything.*

As the business unit's human resources manager, I had a front row seat to the battle between the vice president and his direct reports. In previous months I also learned a thing or two (and pity that it was only a thing or two). From these lessons learned, I recommended to the new vice president that he sponsor an organizational assessment of the division.

He took me up on my offer. The assessment was duly completed and forwarded for his review. Most of the report's findings and recommendations were centered on the four distinct cultures in the division. After digesting the recommendations, the vice president asked whether I was willing to lead a change initiative that would replace the disparate cultures with a single division-level culture.

I said, "Yes."

He hired me away from the human resources department and assigned me the task of creating a new division. The vice president was no longer my internal client, he was now my boss, and his directors were my peers. As director of the new division, my primary goals were to create a strategic plan; align the department's goals, resources, and activities with the change plan; and integrate four cultures into one. It would require a huge organizational change effort.

About a year into this culture change initiative, I had made progress with the staff support managers (those managers responsible for implementing staff rather than operational projects and initiatives). However, I had not made much progress with their supervisors, the division directors who were my peers.

Some seeds of change had been sown, but they had not yet borne much fruit. And no wonder! The directors would routinely approve change initiatives discussed in the V.P.'s staff meetings. But when it came to implementing them, the directors quietly exercised their pocket vetoes. Having declared their agreement, they refused to authorize the staff and/or dollars needed to support the initiatives.

Clearly the directors did not want to publicly oppose the changes supported by the vice president. Nonetheless, they thwarted his initiatives. Staff support managers recognized the tactic and looked to me for help. My title was not Leader of the Change from Four Organizations to One, but everyone recognized me as the de facto change agent. Therefore, everyone assumed the vice president was holding me most accountable for making the change. Their assumptions were soon shaken.

"Shooting" the Change Messenger

During the closing Q & A session of a leadership off-site focusing primarily on change, one of the managers asked who was accountable for the effort. The vice president responded that all of the directors were responsible as a team. The manager followed up by asking whether there was a team captain.

"No," came the reply.

There were several more unsuccessful attempts to get the vice president to say that on his team of equals one person (yours truly) was more equal than the others where the change mission was concerned. Everyone knew I had been hired to lead a division specifically created to implement a culture change. I was the sole point of contact for the consultant hired to advise to that end, and I was the person the vice president held accountable for developing the change initiatives.

To say publicly that I was not the team captain for change was to announce that I lacked authority to overcome any resistance raised by my peers. In hindsight, I understand how the vice president's stance contributed to the development of a team culture; but at the time it was painful, humiliating, and embarrassing. It felt as if my stars had been ripped off my shoulders in public.

More importantly, I felt that the chances of making the mandated change had been diminished. When I was hired the chances were good. When the directors began exercising their pocket vetoes the chances plummeted to poor. Now they were reduced to the proverbial "Slim and None"...and Slim had just been sent packing.

The most influential leaders in the organization other than the vice president made the all-too-human decision to continue working in ways that had made them successful throughout their careers. Why should they switch to unfamiliar approaches advanced by a vice president whose total knowledge of their culture was less than that packed in their respective pinkies?

Their unspoken answer was that they should not—and now I lacked the backing to change their minds. At best, I was back to square one. It was not that I was naïve. I knew that whatever progress had been made had little to do with my brilliance. The directors were picking and choosing when to follow their vice president. Surely, they were picking and choosing which of my initiatives to support, based primarily on the attention they paid to our boss, who stood behind me. Now it appeared that our boss was no longer standing behind me. Whatever influence I had with my peers seemed to be drained away.

Here's the good news: *the lack of positional authority is fatal to change agents only when they rely on positional power to make change happen.* There remains the matter of influence, and influence is powerful. The key to exercising influence without positional power is found in one of my favorite leadership proverbs: *People follow only leaders they trust; they trust only people they know.*

For all of the interaction I had with my peers, they still did not trust me. Their lack of trust was partly because they did not know me. Shortly thereafter, one of my change initiatives was implemented. It called for mandatory leadership cross-training assignments for the department directors and senior managers. Two of my peers and I were on cross-training assignments at the same time.

I was assigned to lead the organization of one of them. The three of us began to interact in different, more personal ways. This allowed us to get to know one another better, which in turn generated more trust, which in turn generated more support for the change initiatives I subsequently sponsored.

The lack of positional authority is painful and costly, but it need not be fatal. If the situation I just described could be salvaged and turned around (and it was!), yours can, too.

Survival Tip for Overcoming a Lack of Positional Authority: *Become Known*

Some years ago I was hired to manage the back office of an organization and change the organization's culture. Prior to the effective date of my hire, I had several conversations with the owner about how I would go about my assignment.

Before my start date, I designed and gained approval for a needs assessment. Call it intuition, common sense, or the hand of God, but I soon realized that I might be pushing too hard too fast. I shelved the needs assessment and decided to focus on "being" rather than "doing."

My first presentation to the management team was not just about work. It was about helping the team to know me better. The presentation included "The Book *on* Greg," in which I shared personal work insights such as: "I ask questions, not as a means of challenging what is being said, but in order to fully understand what is being said." Some personal insights were humorous, such as my declared belief that "If it ain't bacon, it ain't breakfast."

The experiences I generated by *being* instead of *doing* helped me to become known and trusted. This approach will help you (as it helped me) to become a trusted leader better able to influence the values, attitudes, and beliefs of people as well as the policies and procedures that govern their work. Without this influence, overcoming the lack of positional authority is virtually impossible. With it, you can overcome almost anything.

Sparking the Change

1. Have you been in the shoes of the newly hired vice president or of the change agent (or both) in the anecdote I shared? What additional dynamics added to

the resistance you faced? How did the change effort go? What new insights might inform future efforts?

2. How might you flip the emotional equation so that the "wounding" you receive from a senior leader does less damage and inspires more personal growth?

3. Assess the degree to which you are known by peers and others involved in your change effort. Does being known make you feel overly vulnerable? Explain.

CHAPTER SIX

LACK OF LEADERSHIP COMMITMENT

Earlier we saw the anger of David's brother Eliab who asked, "Why did you come down here?" (1 Sam. 17:28). David discovered that change agents are not always warmly received. The fact is that even the warmest welcome cannot ensure active support. Oh, leaders might cheer new initiatives and pledge their backing, but change agents often find it difficult or impossible to collect on those pledges.

Ask me how I know.

The disconnect between warm welcomes and active support is common. I learned about it when the leader of an organization asked for my help in developing a new strategic plan. His hope was to replace the multiple unrelated strategies floating through his organization with a single unifying one. The strategic initiative was part of an overall organizational change effort.

Mistake number one was that the leader asked me to help him rather than his management team. I did as I was asked and worked diligently to develop the plan. When it was rolled out to the management team it was publicly embraced, but not supported.

The first clue got past me. It came when a two-hour session to solicit feedback from the management team took less than twenty minutes. The resistance was on. It came in the form of silence.

Months later, the strategic plan had been fleshed out with individual initiatives. The plan was good, but could not succeed without active support from the leaders. None of the initiatives were well implemented. Some were not implemented at all. The senior leader and I formed the head of the spear, but no one followed, at least not in earnest.

I felt like Caleb, the leader of one of Israel's twelve tribes. After they escaped slavery in Egypt, Moses led the tribes to the brink of the Promised Land and sent twelve leaders to scout out the place.[15] Upon their return, the leaders confirmed that the Promised Land was even better than they had imagined. But they also reported some challenges. There were fearsome people and fortified cities in the land. Ten of the twelve leaders urged Moses and the people to give up on the Promised Land altogether.

> "Shared commitment to change develops only with collective capability to build shared aspirations."
>
> — Peter Senge, *The Dance of Change*

Not Caleb. He advocated going in and taking the place *at once.* Only Joshua stood with him; Caleb received no other active support. The other ten leaders won the argument. They convinced the children of Israel to disobey God and return to Egyptian enslavement.

The resistance to change can be *that* fierce! The cost is fierce, too. The leader-led rebellion caused the children of Israel to wander unnecessarily for forty years.

Like Caleb, I had pointed out a way forward. In my case, the Promised Land was first quartile performance in both customer service and costs. I

---

[15] See the Book of Numbers, chapters 13 and 14.

wasn't asking leaders to fight any physical battles; I merely asked them to support a strategic plan.

I received little support.

The situation I describe can be deadly to your change effort, but it does not have to be. *The lack of support for a change plan is fatal only when change agents forget that the goal is not the successful implementation of the plan, but successfully moving the organization toward its desired state.*

First Things First

Eventually, I developed enough smarts to recognize two key points:

> 1. No matter how great a plan is, it needs support to be successful.
>
> 2. Changing the organization for the better is more important than implementing "my" plan.

Something had to change for change to work. So I led a meeting with the other directors (but without our boss) to take another look at the strategic plan. Having recognized the mistake of not first getting buy-in for the plan, I approached this meeting differently. The goal was not plan improvement, but consensus-building.

In the absence of our boss, leaders were more forthcoming. They added three new areas of focus to the plan and decided to pursue short-term measures of success rather than long-range goals. From a strategic standpoint, I did not believe that either of these decisions improved the plan. But they did produce the buy-in that was lacking the first time.

In some ways, the meeting was painful for me. In my opinion, the original strategic plan created alignment between mission, vision, long-range goals, strategies, annual goals, and specific initiatives. The plan also aligned organizations with diverse areas of responsibility. These features supported the overall organizational culture change plan.

I truly believed that the changes made to the plan by the leaders made alignment in the short-term and success in the long run harder to achieve. Yet I realized that agreement was even more important than the finer points of the strategy. "My" plan had to be sacrificed for a greater good—a plan everyone could buy into.

My change in perspective broke the stalemate. From that point on, each of the directors supported individual initiatives more actively. This step proved to be critical in achieving a successful culture change for the organization. It also helped me to see that it was wrong-headed and—yes— egotistical to think that the leaders' changes made alignment harder. The reality was that none of the change plan would have succeeded had I refused some revision to "my" strategic plan.

Survival Tip for Overcoming a Lack of Leadership Commitment: *Gain Trust*

When you put the organization and its people ahead of your pet plans, good things happen. One of the compliments I treasure most was received during a senior management off-site I facilitated in which managers debated how best to implement organizational change initiatives.

One manager looked me in the eye and said, "I don't believe in this organizational change crap, but I believe in you. And because you believe in it, I am willing to go along with it." I value the compliment to this day. But I assure you; it was hard won and resulted from years of trustworthy behavior. Still, the manager's trust went a long way.

We have already explored trust's prerequisite, which is to become known. Once you are known, trust can be earned by consistently caring for individuals, putting the purpose of the organization first, keeping commitments, and proving on a daily basis that you are who you say you are.

Consistency is key. Part-time trustworthiness won't cut it. To be a successful change agent, you must earn trust on a full-time basis.

Sparking the Change

1. How does Caleb's story speak to yours? What past "enslavement" seems attractive to members of your organization? What changes for the better are they willing to forsake?

2. Have you tried to implement a plan without first winning buy-in? Did you mistake compliance for the buy-in you needed? Explain how, and what it cost the change effort.

3. Is ironclad devotion to your strategic plan short-circuiting your hopes of long-term success? What

rationale might be blinding you to the greater needs of the organization?

CHAPTER SEVEN

LACK OF ENTHUSIASTIC SUPPORT

Employees who are the intended beneficiaries of change tend to welcome the news that it is coming. They are supportive of change and they cheer for it. What they will rarely do is get into the game, at least not right away.

For the first few months after a change initiative is launched, employees stand on the sidelines and wait for something good to happen. Then they wait to see if the good thing lasts. Meanwhile, the change agent is on his or her own.

Nobody followed David into battle; he faced Goliath on his own. "So it was, when the Philistine arose and came and drew near to meet David, that David hurried and ran toward the army to meet the Philistine" (1 Sam. 17:48). Everyone else stood on the sidelines and watched!

In one of my change assignments, employees clearly desired a better work environment. The one they knew was dominated by external compliance requirements and internal procedures. They were not held directly accountable for their actions. Instead, unwanted behaviors were addressed by creating more rules. Prohibition and punishment were the governors of employee conduct.

My assignment was to replace a rules-driven work environment with a more relationship-driven one. Of course, the desired environment had to be defined by the people who would work in it—the employees.

One change initiative included asking employees to identify the values they most wanted to see in their workplace. The initiative began by asking employees to read a book they received about workplace culture. Over the course of two months, selected chapters of the book were opened for group discussion.

Rather than asking employees to adopt the values mentioned by the author, I structured several exercises in which they were free to say which of the four values—better communication, valuing people, accountability, and respect—were most important to them.

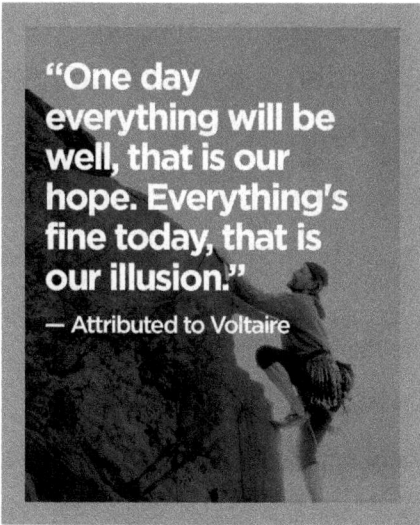

"One day everything will be well, that is our hope. Everything's fine today, that is our illusion."
— Attributed to Voltaire

Although better communication was chosen as the highest value, the meetings I designed to solicit input and generate discussion were stilted. Typically, only one or two employees engaged in what the group wanted more of: communication. Activities tailored to bring people together failed to do so. Few employees showed up unless food was involved, and efforts to build an online community largely fell flat.

While few people expressed satisfaction with the status quo, even fewer people seemed willing to take part in changing it. Yet, directly and indirectly (and behind closed doors) I was encouraged by people to keep trying and keep bucking the system.

Motivated from Within

The situation reminded me of the movie *Cool Hand Luke.* The main character, Luke, is a prisoner on a work farm run by a sadistic warden and some equally cruel guards who delight in dehumanizing inmates. Luke is also a rebel whose subtle and not-so-subtle acts challenge the warden, the guards, and the system. Among his rebellious moves are several escape attempts.

Luke's fellow inmates hope that Luke can spark change in their environment. They egg him on (if you've seen the movie, you get the pun). What they don't do is join in his establishment-challenging escapades.

Toward the end of the movie Luke suffers the brutal consequences of his disobedience. When the prisoners try bringing him back to health, Luke discerns that they want to revive him for their sakes, not his. They have pinned all their hopes on their token rebel; the realization causes him to shout, "Stop feedin' off me."[16]

While my emotions did not descend into despair or resentment during my assignment, I did feel like I was carrying the hopes of people who only secretly cheered me on. The lack of positive reinforcement during meetings and the dearth of visible support from the beneficiaries of the change were demoralizing—especially in light of the other challenges I faced.

As my other day-to-day responsibilities piled up, the competition for my time intensified and I was tempted to assign a lower priority to my change agent role. To justify my actions I borrowed a saying I'd heard: "I am not going to be more invested in your success than you are."

Still, I didn't give up on the change. More importantly, I didn't give up on the people. I loved them and wanted to help fulfill the desires of their hearts for a better work environment. I could not lay blame or give up because their reticence was only part

---

[16] Donn Pearce and Frank R. Pierson, *Cool Hand Luke,* Jalem Productions, 1967, quote cited by IMDb, http://www.imdb.com/title/tt0061512/quotes?ref_=tt_ql_3 (accessed September 4, 2014).

of the success equation. *The lack of visible support from the beneficiaries of change is fatal only when change agents are dependent upon beneficiaries for motivation.*

The key is to be self-authorizing. I learned the concept from Robert Quinn's book, *Deep Change*.[17] For self-authorized change agents, the motivation to pursue the organization's vision is not based on monetary incentives or the desire for professional advancement. Rather, the motivation is based on something internal: the change agent's strong belief in the efficacy of the vision. Support and affirmation are appreciated but not required for the change agent to push through difficult periods.

David did not run to fight Goliath for the incentives offered by King Saul. David battled the giant to demonstrate that his God was bigger than any challenge to His authority, no matter how big the challenger was.

In my case, a key aspect of the change vision (a more relationship-driven workplace) and my affinity

---

[17] Robert E. Quinn, *Deep Change: Discovering the Leader Within* (San Francisco: Jossey-Bass, 1996).

for the people were the primary motivating factors. These ideals contributed to my self-authorization. As a result, I was able to overcome the temptation to be de-motivated by the lack of visible support from the change initiative's intended beneficiaries.

Similarly, self-authorized change agents do not become de-motivated by those who are critical of their change efforts. Unfortunately, being de-motivated and being demoralized are two different things. As I already confessed, I was sometimes demoralized during this assignment. Being self-authorized (i.e., internally motivated) helped me survive periods of demoralization.

Survival Tip for a Lack of Enthusiastic Support: *Give People Something to Do*

It has been said that people support only the change they help create. If the beneficiaries of the change you are tasked to produce do not actively support it, consider giving them a part to play.

In one of my change assignments, I gave the intended beneficiaries a way to invest in the initiative: I created subcommittees to look into issues that affected them. Most often the teams were very small— just two or three people plus me. My role was only to facilitate the meetings. The other committee members spearheaded the development of content and outcomes. As they reported out to the larger group (a role I would have otherwise played), more and more people became engaged and visibly supportive of the change efforts.

Give your intended beneficiaries a stake in the change process and they will invest themselves in the outcome. Score that a win-win!

Sparking the Change

1. What is the importance of having your intended beneficiaries define the initiative's outcomes? What might the process of definition look like in a current or recent assignment?

2. Describe your most recent reaction when encouraged to "keep trying" or "keeping bucking the system." How did the level of your encouragers' active participation color your response? What does your answer reveal?

3. Map out your motives in initiating a current or recent organizational culture change. How are your

motives defining your performance? Are they self-limiting or self-authorizing?

CHAPTER EIGHT

LACK OF CLEAR VISION FROM THE TOP

At times senior leaders are dismayed by the progress of change or the lack thereof. The stalemate between Israel and Goliath affected King Saul this way, and probably caused him to yield to young David's offer to fight the giant.

Scripture describes what Saul was up against:

The Philistine said, "I defy the armies of Israel this day; give me a man, that we may fight together." When Saul and all Israel heard these words of the Philistine, they were dismayed and greatly afraid (1 Samuel 17:10-11).

One of the best examples of culture change I have been a part of was led by a group called Culture Change Consultants, a firm that specialized in modifying company culture to reduce the number of on-the-job injuries.

All caring companies aspire to this noble goal. However, the vast majority of companies try to reach it through a combination of engineering, equipment, and educational strategies. Change Consultants advocated and supported an approach that reached beyond these "Three E's." They focused on developing an environment rich with the values, attitudes, beliefs, and behaviors that are displayed by organizations whose culture of safety is emphasized.

As the director in my business unit who was responsible for safety, I drew on this approach to create a high-level strategic plan suitable for the assignment. When developing any strategic plan, I start by asking and answering an essential question: *What is this strategy supposed to accomplish?*

In the particular organization whose culture we were trying to change, the traditional answer in prior years would have been: *The strategy is supposed to reduce the number of injuries by x percent.* It was a common objective, with the numeric target varying according to conditions.

However, this traditional approach was now discarded. The safety culture we wanted to create would report *zero injuries.* The idea was that no injury is acceptable. Such a goal is laudable but seemed impossible. The culture change needed to replace traditional, numerically-based goals (to reduce injuries by certain percentages) with goals that were values-based was huge.

Clearly, the answer to my essential strategy question had to be tailored to create a culture of safety in which *zero injuries* was the eventual outcome. The strategy was as follows:

> Create and sustain a work environment that values:
>
> - Having every employee leave the workplace unhurt
>
> - Using work behaviors and practices that uncompromisingly protect everyone's safety
>
> - Caring for the safety of one's fellow employees

- Stopping work whenever unsafe conditions or behaviors are observed, until the job can be completed safely

Leading an effort that asks employees to relinquish familiar values, attitudes, beliefs, and behaviors is more than difficult, even when those ideals have generated less than desirable conditions. The consultant duly warned the firm that such a

> "Mythic leaders...a very special group of individuals who combine extraordinary clarity of vision and a single-minded sense of purpose to excite, energize, and win the loyalty of large groups of people."
> — David A. Nadler, *Champions of Change*

culture change would take five to seven years. The leaders' vision would have to take this time frame into account.

Sure enough, less than two years into the process, some senior leaders threatened to dump the change initiatives. They were no longer apt to convey a clear sense of vision from the top.

Taking Heart

For the people implementing the change, this news was extremely disheartening. Some of the initiatives were just starting to have an impact. Frontline employees were engaging with the plan and a number of values-based behavior changes had emerged.

Just as the change began to show signs of life, some senior leaders were ready to abandon it. They felt that the safety statistics were not dropping sharply enough. Ironically, reducing the reliance on statistics to measure success was one of the changes being pursued. Yet this group of leaders was still more keyed into numbers than into values. Their vision wavered, so like King Saul, they were dismayed.

The dismay filtered through the ranks. Some departments implemented command and control initiatives that emphasized public accountability sessions. A few of the corporate officers began to challenge not only the change, but the change agents as well.

I grumbled (to myself, of course), "True change begins at the top and it's time for true change." It seemed ironic to me that those who desired the change, hired the change consultants, and personally launched the change initiative were now abandoning the mission. I thought, "If the results two years into a five- to seven-year process can tempt them to quit doing the hard work that's needed, why should I or any of us be willing to do it?" It seemed easier to quit than to champion a change that would not mollify high-level executives.

Certainly, senior leadership threatening to pull the plug can be fatal to the change initiative. However, it need not be fatal to the change itself. Robert Quinn describes transformational leaders who are willing to champion the cause under such conditions, saying they "still care enough to be willing to be punished for doing what it takes to save the organization."[18]

When some elements of senior leadership show a lack of commitment and clear vision, change agents can nurture the seeds of change already planted. They can sow more seeds of change even as their larger, more formal change initiatives lose support. Therefore, I lobbied hard to keep the change initiative

---

[18] Robert E. Quinn, *Deep Change: Discovering the Leader Within* (San Francisco: Jossey-Bass, 1996), 127.

alive at the larger organizational level, and I supported the change agents in individual work units.

Was this insubordination? No. The safety culture change initiatives were not forbidden; they just weren't supported. I supported small guiding coalitions that continued to pursue new ideas reflecting the principles of the change, even if they did not carry an official change label.

The withdrawal of support *was* disheartening, but it did not have to stop the heart of progress. The shape of the mission changed, but the organization continued to move toward the safety culture.

TAKING SAUL'S "TEMPERATURE"

How mercurial is the senior leader involved in your change assignment? Is this leader's dismay reasonable or part of a roller coaster ride that was underway long before you arrived? King Saul had issues. Everyone has issues. Before you throw in the towel, learn what drives the senior leader out of your corner. Address any issues behind the issue. Then stand strong and complete your assignment.

Survival Tip for a Lack of Clear Vision from the Top: *Manage Up*

Just because the senior leader stops speaking out in support of the change initiative does not mean the leader's continued silence is inevitable. You can still create opportunities for the leader to speak in support of the change.

In an initiative that included improving the work environment, I mentioned to the organization's leader how much weight his words carried with his employees. Unfortunately, his busy schedule kept him from being a highly visible leader. When he did address staffers, however, he spoke mostly about how to improve the organization. I shared with him news about the good things that were going on. This enabled him to praise specific employees for specific examples of their good work.

This senior leader appreciated being made aware of details that were otherwise invisible to him. Even though he did not fully realize it, his public praise made him a contributor to the change in work environment.

Empower the senior leaders with whom you collaborate and they will even inadvertently contribute to the clear vision they previously failed to provide.

Sparking the Change

1. When has devotion to familiar values, attitudes, beliefs, and behaviors blocked progress toward new ones that all parties agreed were more desirable? What about that resistance surprised or most stymied your efforts?

2. How "infectious" is a leader's lack of vision clariy? How infectious is that leader's dismay? How does the "virus" motivate or de-motivate you as the change agent?

3. You can encourage and empower a vision-challenged senior leader to speak for the cause. How else can you inspire such a leader to contribute to the mission?

CHAPTER NINE

MISUNDERSTANDING OWNERSHIP

David and Saul both wanted Goliath's head, but their approaches differed. "Saul gave David his own armor—a bronze helmet and a coat of mail. David put it on, strapped the sword over it, and took a step or two to see what it was like, for he had never worn such things before" (1 Sam. 17:38-39a NLT).

"I can hardly move!" David exclaimed, as he removed the ill-fitting gear.[19]

Like David, our notions of how to implement change usually differ from those of our senior leaders. We can easily get carried away with our opinions and successes and find ourselves at odds with those who truly own the change.

We touched on the misunderstanding of ownership briefly in our earlier survey of friendly fire sources. As if their role weren't tough enough, change agents make it more difficult by confusing accountability with ownership. The error is understandable; it is also unforced. Although they are typically held somewhat accountable for the outcomes of change initiatives, change agents are not crowned as the owners of change. The real owners are the senior leaders to whom change agents report.

The confusion usually begins in the middle of the change process. The senior leader becomes less visible while the change agent amasses support from leaders and employees and makes measurable progress.

> "Sometimes it's not enough to know what things mean; sometimes you have to know what things don't mean."
> — Bob Dylan

Invariably, a critical decision of substantial impact to the change effort comes due. Not surprisingly, the leader and the change agent see the decision differently. When the king of the change says: "Wear my armor," the agent of change protests that armor will impede the plan.

---

[19] See First Samuel 17:39b.

Because senior leaders are the rightful owners of the initiative, they have final say. Often their decisions seem to undercut the change agent's efforts, at least partly because they take broader issues into account. Always, their decisions are made in ways that remind change agents who is really in charge.

Take It in Stride

The realization that leaders continue in their unilateral authority (despite the change initiatives they endorse) can be devastating to change agents. It is also instructive. Whether or not decisions from above support the change they have worked to implement, they learn that being accountable and being in charge are not the same thing.

Yes, change agents exercise influence in the change process; but they are "shepherds" in the story. Like David, they must value their rightful roles and not choose to become "kings." It so happens that David won the armor decision. But change agents don't typically win these calls. More often than not, they leave the negotiation with orders they would rather not follow.

One of my assignments seemed to be the exception. The senior leader publicly declared that he had asked me to lead the change while he focused on more entrepreneurial aspects of the business.

His decision made sense. Business was good primarily because of a technologically savvy field operations manager. He was an excellent individual contributor, and the organization relied heavily on his strong command of the subject matter. He saved the firm significant amounts of money, created new ways of working, and generated additional revenue.

There was just one catch: the savvy individual contributor was less skilled as a team player. In a culture that was moving toward team orientation, his self-reliance subverted the change process. His less-than-stellar people skills also sent other talented people running for cover. They felt intimidated into being silent at meetings and were hesitant to offer up new ideas.

The leader of the organization finally decided to reassign the manager. However, the search process was extraordinarily long and ended without identifying a qualified replacement. So the leader and I discussed next steps. I was ready to revamp the search process. But rather than continue the process, the leader declared, "This is not working!" Frustrated, he reinstated the self-reliant manager.

I was stunned and ready to quit. "Not working?" I thought. "Of course it's not working! There's a major roadblock that you refuse to move."

Bang! I had suffered a self-inflicted wound *because I thought I was running things.* The leader's unexpected decision reminded me that I was not. Worse, I had not seen the hit coming. As one change expert put it, "It's not the surprises in life that are so debilitating. The truly crushing force is being surprised that you are surprised."[20]

Even self-inflicted wounds sting, but they need not be life-threatening. *They are fatal only when change agents are unwilling to conform their behavior to*

---

[20] Daryl R. Connor, *Managing at the Speed of Change* (New York: Random House, 1993), 28.

reality by accepting their role as leaders of change rather than leaders of organizations.

This is about managing expectations, something change agents do every day. They help correct the unrealistically high expectations of change beneficiaries, knowing that unmet expectations can cause change initiatives to lose steam, or worse. When the expectations of the beneficiaries are too low, change agents know what they will say: "Nothing will really be different, so why am I spending so much time in meetings about changing things?" Low expectations can make the change effort seem unworthy of beneficiaries' participation.

Both scenarios are difficult to manage. Yet the most important expectations change agents must manage are their own! Not confusing accountability with ownership is a big part of this important task.

Make the Most of *Your* Role

The identity of *owner* does not belong to the change agent. That is reality. However, change agents must do more than acknowledge reality. They must make the best of it. Even when friendly fire strikes, change agents remain accountable for making their efforts as successful as possible. Those who accept this accountability are better able to survive the fallout from ownership decisions that seem counterproductive to the change initiative.

For me, this acceptance required an attitude adjustment. I had been given so much autonomy in my assignment that I assumed the attitude of an owner. Like the seagulls in the movie *Nemo,* I flew around crying, "Mine. Mine. Mine. Mine."[21]

I had to come in for a landing and remember the beginning, including why I had signed on to the change initiative. I had to remember the respect I had for the senior leader and the reason I was glad to be working on his behalf. He had a vision for the organization that I believed in. I needed to support it.

My true belief in the vision had produced what began as healthy self-authorizing behaviors. When combined with the autonomy delegated by the senior leader, however, my self-authorization morphed into

[21] "Finding Nemo Quotes," IMDb, http://www.imdb.com/title/tt0266543/quotes?ref_=tt_ql_3 (accessed August 23, 2014).

delusions of ownership. Revisiting my belief in the leader's vision and reminding myself of his confidence in me helped me to adjust my attitude and realize who was working for whom.

The adjustment also afforded me increased clarity regarding the senior leader's vision for the change. I understood better what he was willing to accept or tolerate during the change implementation. The bonus was that I also realized I had become invested in someone else's garden to the unhealthy degree that I spent my personal time tending it. Once my attitude was set right, I redirected some personal time to my own projects.

Now I had an added outlet for my desire to produce results, and the fruit of my labor had a new place to bloom—my own garden!

Survival Tip for Understanding Ownership: *Stay in Touch with the Leader*

More than once, I have wounded myself by confusing accountability with ownership. Now making sure I have regular meetings with senior leaders helps me to avoid the pitfall.

Even if you are capable of acting without the decision-making of the senior leader (the leader's *active participation* is always encouraged, by the way), resist the opportunity to go it alone. Continue to hold regular meetings. If the senior leader does not reach out to you, then you do the reaching out. It will save both of you some very big headaches.

Because of the nature of the relationship, these meetings naturally center on work issues. However, make a point of carving out some time for personal discussion. Senior leaders are not just colleagues; they are people. When this approach becomes mutual, trust is built and maintained—and role confusion is eliminated.

Sparking the Change

1. Being granted the "perfect" level of autonomy in the change initiative is an unreasonable expectation. Which assignment came closest to hitting your "sweet spot" in this regard? Which seemed farthest from the mark? Are your answers more reflective of a senior leader's attitudes, or of yours?

2. How willing are you to take senior leadership decisions in stride? How has your level of willingness played out in your career?

3. Describe the senior leader with whom you are working as a person rather than a colleague. What does he or she mean to you? Does this leader deserve more honor than you are currently giving? Explain.

PART III
THE CHANGE
AGENT'S
ARSENAL

CHAPTER TEN

TECHNICAL SKILL

Weapons Are Important, Too

We have seen ways to navigate very challenging situations, including overcoming friendly fire. By itself, overcoming friendly fire cannot guarantee success. It merely positions change agents to succeed. Being in position is one thing: winning the "battle" is quite another.

I am reminded of one of the closing scenes in the Civil War movie, *Glory*[22] in which a battalion of Union soldiers is asked to mount a frontal assault on a coastal Confederate fort. All previous efforts had failed, but the battalion, which happens to be comprised mostly of black troops, demonstrates great heroism and pushes back the Confederate front line.

Eventually, some of the troops and a white officer reach the top of an embankment. For a moment everyone believes the battle has been won. But as the troops look down the incline, they see more Confederate troops and more cannons. Great progress has been made, but the battle is not yet over. The Union battalion must rise to the occasion using every weapon at its disposal.

Using our "weapons" well is what we are about to explore. The story of David and Goliath provides insight once again—this time for change agents who have overcome internal challenges but have yet to tackle the challenges

> **"Without the right skills and attitudes, people feel disempowered."**
> — John P. Kotter, *Leading Change*

of change itself. A short excerpt from the story lists the weapons at David's disposal:

> Then he took his staff in his hand; and he chose for himself five smooth stones from the brook, and put them in a shepherd's bag, in a pouch which he had, and his sling was in his hand.

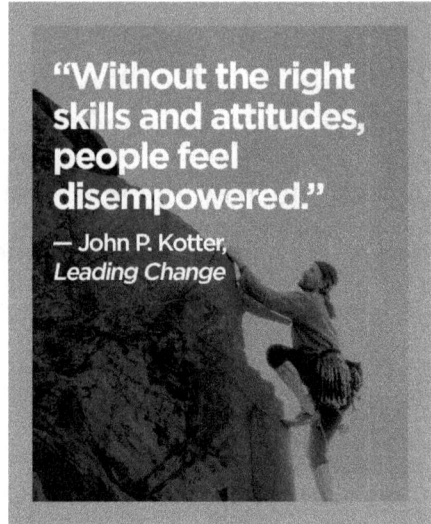

---

[22] *Glory*, released by TriStar Pictures, 1989.

And he drew near to the Philistine (1 Samuel 17:40).

As important as David's sling was in transforming pebbles into weapons, we will focus on his staff and the stones. David did not approach Goliath empty-handed. Likewise, change agents must approach the change Goliath with *their* weapons. This chapter and each of the next five chapters covers one weapon.

Let's begin with the staff—not a team of people in this case, but the strong piece of wood crafted for the shepherd's use in the field, and our metaphor for *technical skill.*

David's Staff—His Skill

In David's time, a staff was "used much like a cane by travelers…but could also serve as a simple weapon, especially in the hands of a shepherd."[23] Three uses stand out and demonstrate the keen skills of shepherds:

---

[23] Herbert Lockyer, Sr., editor, *Nelson's Bible Dictionary* (Nashville: Thomas Nelson Publishers, 1986), s.v. "staff."

1. During lambing season, the shepherd worked to keep lambs with their mothers. Touching the lambs would cause ewes to reject their young. Using the staff to keep them together required a "very deft maneuver."[24]

2. The staff was used to pull in lambs for inspection.[25] A good shepherd had to be acquainted with the condition of his flock.

3. Sheep are prone to wandering. The shepherd jabbed and nudged them to keep them from getting lost.[26]

David knew his sheep and their needs. He was also savvy in the art of using his staff to shepherd them. Change agents must also be savvy. For them, the "staff" is their technical skill and the overall ability to produce results. Just as the shepherd's good intentions are not enough to care for his flock, the

---

[24] John Ritenbaugh, "Bible Verses about Shepherd's Staff Used for Inspection," *Forerunner Commentary,* Bible Tools, http://www.bibletools.org/index.cfm/fuseaction/Topical.show/RTD/cgg/ID/14587/Shepherds-Staff-Used-for-Inspection.htm (accessed August 23, 2014).
[25] Ibid.
[26] Ibid.

good intentions of change agents are not enough to complete their assignments. Facilitating an organization's culture change requires skill—both to overcome the friendly fire from within and to lead the organization and its people down the difficult path of change.

Change agents must understand and function within the role assigned to them. They must also be consciously aware of opportunities to grow. If becoming known to your collaborators is uncomfortable, be determined to take more risks along those lines. If humility is not your strong suit, treat the challenges you face as opportunities to learn. If friendly fire often takes you by surprise, cultivate greater awareness of its sources.

Your technical skills are equally important in shepherding a successful change initiative, and in surviving the effort. Keep your skills sharp and keep improving. Look for opportunities to grow and mentor others in your skills. Your "staff" will give you something solid to lean upon.

Next, we will explore the five stones: experience, belief in the vision, tenacity, courage, and self-preservation.

Survival Tip for Winning the "War": *Know and Use Your Weapons*

No capable army goes to battle without its weapons, and no soldier in a capable army arrives on the front lines without first being trained to use them. David took his staff and selected five smooth stones. Then, with his sling, he launched a single stone to defeat the enemy. The shepherd was also a skilled defender.

David's amazing marksmanship was no accident and the battle with Goliath was not his first "rodeo." He had learned to defend his flock and to conquer fierce predators in the open fields. He had no doubt practiced for years, launching hundreds or thousands of stones so that, when the time came, his accuracy would be dead-on.

Everything you have learned has prepared you for your current role. Use your technical skills to their best advantage and they will serve your larger purpose as a change agent—to facilitate the culture transformation that benefits the organizations you serve.

Sparking the Change

1. Have you mistaken a victory in battle for the end of war? What did the miscalculation cost you and your mission? Why is the misread so easy to make?

2. Which of your skills are most well-honed? Where can you improve? What might growth in this area mean to current and future missions?

3. Your relational skills are valuable, but are you over-reliant on them? Is there a gap in your technical skills that is prompting the imbalance? How can you remedy the challenge?

CHAPTER ELEVEN

EXPERIENCE

The first of the five "stones" is *experience,* one of the primary weapons in the change agent's arsenal. Experience produces confidence; it was one of the reasons David was so sure he could battle Goliath successfully. When Saul pointed out Goliath's prowess as a warrior, David shared his own resumé:

> Your servant used to keep his father's sheep, and when a lion or a bear came and took a lamb out of the flock, I went out after it and struck it, and delivered the lamb from its mouth; and when it arose against me, I caught it by its beard, and struck and killed it. Your servant has killed both lion and bear; and this uncircumcised Philistine will be like one of them, seeing he has defied the armies of the living God (1 Samuel 17:34-36).

Fresh off my own experience as the change agent for a vice president's effort to create a single organizational culture from several, I was asked to lead a relatively new operations organization.

Having once been part of a different, larger organization, the newly detached one was transferred to my division. However, it came without director-level leadership and its senior manager reported directly to the vice president. Eight months after the transfer, I was asked to provide that director-level leadership.

It was clear that a culture change was in order. The group's former colleagues were now their largest internal clients. Unfortunately, the group's values, attitudes, and beliefs revealed how they saw themselves: as somewhat subservient order-takers rather than the providers of a valuable service. An informal survey of their colleagues-turned-clients confirmed the organizational "self-image." The clients' sentiments were notably negative; my new group was not highly regarded or well-respected.

> "Commitment is time-consuming and expensive to attain. But once its infrastructure develops, the speed of assimilation can accelerate."
>
> — Daryl R. Connor, *Managing at the Speed of Change*

Catering to clients had not produced a good relationship.

Lesson Learned

Based on what I learned from the survey and my own discussions with the directors and managers of the client organization, I developed a change initiative. In this case, I would serve as both leader and change agent. However, I did so with the benefit of experience from my previous assignment. Even the experiences I would like to have forgotten proved valuable; I put the lessons I learned to good use.

Although I was eager to get started, I did not launch the change effort until the person chosen as the initiative's project manager became available. The delay amounted to several weeks. I had learned from experience that it was better to launch a well-prepared effort a little later than an ill-prepared one sooner.

Despite the negativity documented by the survey, I shared a summary of the results with the managers and supervisors. I also took accountability for the outcome (and tried to protect the confidence of the group) by admitting that my self-imposed delay in transitioning the organization from start-up to operational mode may have contributed to the clients' feelings.

The managers and supervisors responded well. They were eager to develop strategies that would improve their standing with their clients. I organized a series of off-sites in which managers and supervisors developed plans to create a new group identity separate from the identity it held in its former division. They also proposed ways to improve their performance in their clients' eyes.

Their development of a value proposition and an action plan to carry it out proved to be among the most effective strategies birthed in the off-sites. This effort took a lot longer than one I mentioned in an earlier chapter. That plan was developed in a vacuum and lacked buy-in. Having learned my lesson well, this plan resulted from group consensus, with buy-in from day one.

The change "took"! A year later, there was an increase in productivity and a decrease in costs. Client satisfaction and my group's self-esteem were much higher.

Experience has its benefits.

Survival Tip for the Experienced: *Apply What You Have Learned*

Experience is always a great teacher, but there is no payoff unless you pay attention. As a change agent, you can become so focused on innovation that you forget to learn from the past. But experiences—bad or good, small or large, brief or extended—are weapons of choice, even when your job is as forward-looking as organizational transformation.

Appropriately rely on *and apply* the lessons you have learned; you and your organization will be well served by them. Do not, however, be too eager to learn from mistakes. Learning from your blunders is good, learning from other people's is better. Ask a more experienced change agent to act as your mentor. Find someone who is willing to be transparent in sharing difficult experiences. Then be humble and transparent enough to take them to heart and use them for your betterment.

Make the most of where you and others have been: apply what you and they have learned.

Sparking the Change

1. What can your current assignment draw from a memorable past experience? Be specific in developing an application. *Then apply it.*

2. Can you describe a circumstance in which waiting for a certain player to come aboard might be the wrong decision? Evaluate the situation's the pros and cons.

3. Describe an assignment in which the intended beneficiaries of the change were stymied by a poor sense of their value to the organization and to clients.

How satisfied or dissatisfied were you with your change effort, and why?

CHAPTER TWELVE

BELIEF IN THE VISION

My first job as an attorney was in a firm that represented management in labor disputes. Having faced many union leaders across the negotiating table, the partners in the law firm saw the leaders falling into two categories: some were *representatives* of the union members; the rest were *real believers* in the ideals of the labor movement.

The firm's partners believed they had a better chance of reaching agreements with representatives than with real believers. Representatives tended to be more pragmatic in speaking for their constituents. Real believers were more idealistic; they were driven by their values and their belief in the tenets of the movement, they spoke for ideas first and foremost.

So it was with David. He was not moved by the circumstances; he was motivated by his belief in an ideal.

David said to the Philistine, "You come to me with a sword, with a spear, and with a javelin.

But I come to you in the name of the Lord of hosts, the God of the armies of Israel, whom you have defied. This day the Lord will deliver you into my hand, and I will strike you and take your head from you. And this day I will give the carcasses of the camp of the Philistines to the birds of the air and the wild beasts of the earth, that all the earth may know that there is a God in Israel" (1 Samuel 17:45-46).

David did not rush to battle for a reward. He did it because he believed his God was greater.

> **"Successful change is rooted in commitment."**
>
> — Daryl R. Connor, *Managing at the Speed of Change*

Like David, change agents are more likely to overcome the challenges of change when they believe in the goals of the change. For true-believing change agents, change is not about them personally; it is about the vision of the organization. Therefore their personal success is not important; the success of the vision is.

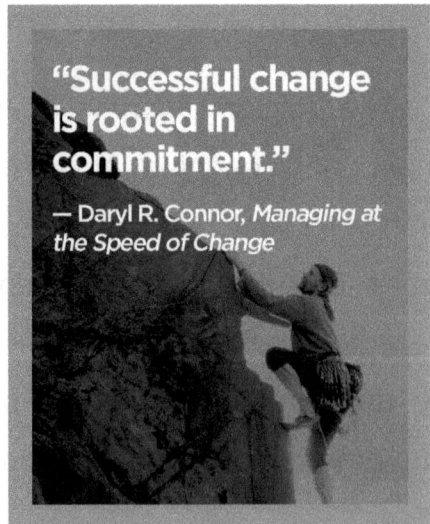

In terms of the work, these change agents don't maintain any identity apart from the organization's vision. They pursue what is right for it over what is right for them or other individuals. Often what is right for the change agent is *not* right for the vision. To say it bluntly: change agents must sometimes take it on the chin for the vision.

Leading with My Chin

In Chapter Five I described a question and answer session that ended painfully for me. It was during an off-site in which middle managers looked for, but did not receive, assurance that I was the de facto leader of the organization's change initiative.

I wrote:

To say publicly that I was not the team captain for change was to announce that I lacked authority to overcome any resistance raised by my peers....it was painful, humiliating, and embarrassing.... More importantly, I felt that the chances of making the mandated change had been diminished.

My ultimate point was that the lack of positional authority is fatal to change agents only when they rely on positional power to make change happen. More influential than positional power is trust; and trust is gained through relationships. However, to establish or enhance relationships, one has to be present, and I wanted to disappear!

As I drove home from the meeting, quitting sounded good. Not only did I believe that my modest amount of influence had been drained away, I believed that those who were resisting change had been emboldened to increase their resistance.

So why did I show up for work bright and early Monday morning? It was because of a question I asked myself while driving home on a winding mountain road. It was very simple: "Do I believe in the change or not?"

My answer was, "Yes," therefore, my next steps became clear. My reputation, my feelings, and the task's level of difficulty were secondary. Because I believed in the change, I was willing to endure whatever was necessary to excel and bring the change to pass.

I have revisited the "Do I believe in the change?" question many times. I did it when an effort to develop more shared annual goals produced one shared goal out of seventeen. I did it when colleagues intentionally violated group agreements. And I did it again when a consensus-driven process to create organizational priorities was disavowed by a key leader because her pet project was further down the list than she liked.

But I also revisited the question when the vice president acknowledged to me, six years after we started, that his vision of one organization (not a collection of groups) led by a senior leadership team (not individual directors) had been achieved.

Belief in the vision goes a long way toward achieving it.

Survival Tip for Believing in the Vision: *Find Fulfillment*

You can't always choose your change assignments. If you could, you would handpick the ones most likely to produce the outcomes in which you believe wholeheartedly. Yet even in those instances when the change initiative is more of an assignment than a crusade, you can find fulfillment.

Change assignments are multifaceted. Even when you are not a real believer in the overall initiative, some aspect of it will probably arouse your passions. Or you might truly believe in the underlying values of the change. If you look for it, you will probably find the true-believing passion to prevail.

Change agents who find a spark of belief when the full sizzle seems lacking are real believers in change itself. If that is you, you will reap the benefits of transformation's red-hot results.

Just stay with it.

Sparking the Change

1. In your current assignment, do you identify more with the *representatives* described in the chapter, or the *real believers?* What facts and/or attitudes underlie your status?

2. Have you led with your chin in the past? Does it seem that you are doing it now? What does it tell you about your approach to change?

3. Is there a positive experience you can revisit when a change effort appears to go sidewise? What is it and why does it encourage you?

CHAPTER THIRTEEN

TENACITY

Vince Lombardi is credited with saying that "the difference between a successful person and others is not a lack of strength, not a lack of knowledge, but rather a lack of will."[27]

David would probably agree with Lombardi. Even if he was a slick hand with a slingshot, David did not prevail over Goliath because he was a proven, experienced soldier. David was a shepherd, and a young shepherd at that.

Yet, he was tenacious.

"Don't worry about this Philistine," David told Saul. "I'll go fight him!" "Don't be ridiculous!" Saul replied. "There's no way you can fight this Philistine and possibly win! You're only a boy, and he's been a man of war since his youth.' But David persisted...." (1 Samuel 17:32-34 NLT).

---

[27] "Vince Lombardi Biography," bio.,
http://www.biography.com/people/vince-lombardi-9385362#synopsis
(accessed August 25, 2014).

Like David and Vince Lombardi, change agents must be tenacious. Change does not happen quickly or quietly. Three to five years is the minimum investment for change. Leaders rarely have the patience to wait

> "If you fell down yesterday, stand up today."
> — H.G. Wells

that long. Even a well-run change effort can be shut down by an impatient leader. The change agent shepherding an "average" initiative faces even more hazards.

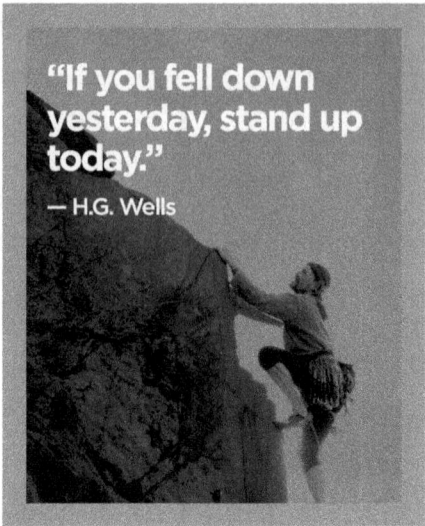

Change agents do well to keep Coach Lombardi's maxim in mind, along with a closely related corollary: "Where there is a will, there is a way."

Tenacity is willingness that persists.

Making Bricks without Straw

When the vice president asked me to lead his division's organizational change effort, he put me in charge of a new organization into which several work groups were transferred. Several other functions were created from scratch. The organization contained several centralized functions helpful to implementing change, including training, communications, organizational development, planning, process management, and information technology.

But over the next eighteen to twenty-four months, the organization was whittled down. The company created a new emphasis on process management and technology and each business unit formed its own process and technology divisions. My business unit formed its process and technology group by transferring those functions to a newly formed stand-alone division.

When the company centralized the communication function, I said good-bye to my communication group. When the human resources business unit centralized the organizational change function, I said so long to my organizational development group. Meanwhile, my boss's new boss shared his affinity for strategic planning. That function was moved to the business unit level.

Each of the four newly centralized functions was designed to meet the needs of the company's divisions. They did, but not completely.

Amidst these changes, what was expected of me did not diminish, although my ability to meet those expectations was pinched. I felt like the children of Israel in the book of Exodus. When Pharaoh was angered by Moses' request to release the Israelite slaves, he ordered them to make bricks without the straw that had previously been provided. The supply was stopped; but the quota of bricks to be produced remained the same.

Although I seemed to be in a similar predicament, I did not see myself as being unable to advance the mission. I no longer directly managed the process, technology, organizational development, or communication functions, and I was no longer the primary driver of department level strategy; but I continued to utilize those functions the best I could.

I formed an alliance with the leader of the process and technology organization, who did her best to meet the needs of my department. The newly centralized corporate communications department assigned someone to my division. I made sure we had regular meetings so that my department's communications needs continued to be met.

My ability to develop integrated and aligned initiatives involving one or more of these functions was diminished, but, like David, I persisted. Then, as strategic planning functions were centralized by the business unit, the scope of my organization's work became so small that I was assigned an operations group to ensure that I was operating at full capacity.

I did what I could; I persisted in pursuing the vision of a single organizational culture. It took a couple of years, but eventually, the vice president realized that he needed a more direct, hands-on approach to the key functions that supported the change. As a result, he gave me the green light to acquire the resources needed to pursue it.

I hired a project manager to lead centralized support projects, such as strategic planning activities (and a newly invigorated communications function). With my boss's blessing, I met with the manager of organizational development in the human resources department and successfully lobbied them to assign someone to support organizational change management activities within the division. I was her single point of contact.

With these resources, the change initiative continued to progress and eventually succeeded. The victory was hard fought, but tenacity paid off.

TENACITY AS GAME-CHANGER

Tenacity is a quality that makes other qualities work better. If I am highly skilled, but quick to throw in the towel, any outlet for my skills will be short-lived. Even if I have the genius of a Michelangelo or Blaise Pascal, a lack of tenacity will trim my list of accomplishments. Tenacity is what keeps change agents in the game when they don't realize the victory is just around the bend. Without tenacity, victory can be forfeited.

Survival Tip in Being Tenacious: *Get Back Up...Again*

Tenacity is not like physical strength. Some people are physically stronger than other, *period*. I'm not the strongest physically. If I were asked to grip a bar and hang in the air with my feet off the ground, I would let go fairly quickly. Physically, I would not wow certain guys at the gym.

But if after I landed on the ground, jumped back up, and gripped the bar again and again and again, they would call me tenacious. I don't have to possess great physical strength to be tenacious. It is a mind-set, and it impacts my performance as a change agent.

Tenacity doesn't mean you never want to quit. Sometimes the change effort is so difficult quitting sounds like a win. I have quit in my mind more than once; but I came back to work the next day. This quitting and coming back might sound like silly mental gymnastics, but it's more than that. Letting go of the bar provides temporary stress relief and forces me to decide. That's when tenacity kicks in and I return to the assignment with increased commitment to the mission.

You don't have to be a physical powerhouse to succeed. The weapon called *tenacity* levels the playing field. You use it every time you bounce back from an "I quit" day.

Sparking the Change

1. What part have impatience and tenacity played in your career? How are they connected? Looking back, how might increased tenacity have changed a specific change outcome?

2. It is easy to get angry when "Pharaoh" makes unreasonable demands. What is your immediate reaction when someone makes your job more difficult? Does your reaction speak about them or about you? How so?

3. How is your level of tenacity affecting the exercise of your technical skills? How is it affecting your belief in the vision?

CHAPTER FOURTEEN

COURAGE

"When we pursue our vision, we must believe that we have enough courage and confidence in ourselves to reach our goal. We must leap into the chasm of uncertainty and strive bravely ahead."[28]

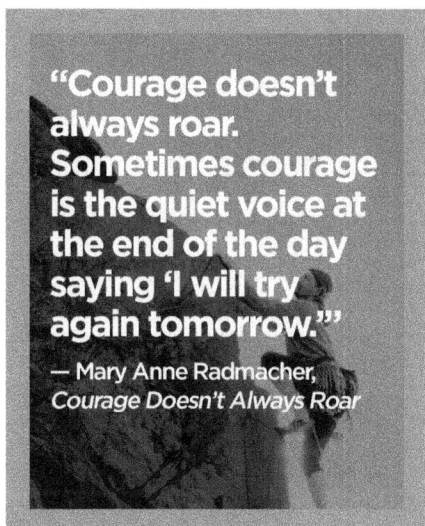

> **"Courage doesn't always roar. Sometimes courage is the quiet voice at the end of the day saying 'I will try again tomorrow.'"**
>
> — Mary Anne Radmacher, *Courage Doesn't Always Roar*

That's exactly what David did; He strove bravely ahead.

"So it was, when the Philistine arose and came and drew near to meet David, that David hurried and ran toward the army to meet the Philistine" (1 Sam. 17:48).

Everyone around David attested to the uncertainty of his chosen mission, but he refused to acquiesce.

---

[28] Robert E. Quinn, *Deep Change: Discovering the Leader Within* (San Francisco: Jossey-Bass, 1996), 84.

The "chasm of uncertainty" can trip up change agents. To hold their footing, they must find the courage to be comfortable with ambiguity, *because* they believe strongly in the change vision. This means running toward the challenges every large-scale change presents. The plight of change agents is to take their opportunities as they come—laced with uncertainty.

I faced such an opportunity in my role as change agent for my church. My boss and I were discussing a change in the group values, attitudes, and beliefs associated with the way the church ran its conferences. As the administrative pastor, one of my responsibilities was managing the four conferences the church hosted each year. For the first conference I managed, I felt right at home. Operational excellence was the primary value, and I knew how to pursue organizational excellence.

I viewed my boss as my client, so one of my primary goals was to make him happy. Making sure that the logistical underpinnings of the conference performed excellently went a long way toward accomplishing this goal.

After the first conference, however, I gave myself a change assignment. Thankfully, it was blessed by my boss—and thankfully, I had courage enough to find that out. The change was to transform group values, attitudes, and beliefs rooted in a performance-driven, rules-based work environment into group values, attitudes, and beliefs that were rooted in a presence-driven, relationship-based environment.

Making the Shift, Internally and Externally

Changing the environment demanded a personal shift where conferences were concerned. My primary client would no longer be my boss. The people who attended the conferences were my primary clients now. Although operational excellence was still important, my goal was to ensure an environment in which attendees would have meaningful encounters with a supernatural God.

The way employees and volunteers approached their conference duties would also have to change. In previous conferences, they focused on ensuring that the rules were followed. When attendees did not follow the rules, staffers and volunteers addressed the breach. This approach was reinforced every time a church leader (including my boss) pointed out a case of rule-breaking and every time an employee or volunteer was reprimanded for breaching or allowing a breach in the rules.

This was a performance-driven approach. I had already noticed performance-driven behavior in the day-to-day work environment, which seemed contrary to what was being preached from the pulpit. So with some fortitude and my boss's concurrence, I launched an initiative to change the culture.

In my second conference experience, I eliminated some of the rules that negatively impacted my clients' ability to enjoy the conference. But to change the underlying culture—the values, attitudes, and beliefs of the employees and volunteers—I had to take additional steps. One step was yet another one-on-one conversation with my boss.

First, I explained the performance-driven environment that shaped the values, attitudes, and beliefs of the employees and volunteers who worked the conferences. That didn't take much courage. But I swallowed hard before the next step: telling my boss about his role in creating the performance-driven environment.

That took courage. It is rare in any environment for employees to inform their bosses that they are part of a problem! In this case, my boss was also my pastor. The way I was raised, presenting such a hypothesis was akin to challenging God, or at least one of His direct reports. Without the courage of my deeply-held conviction that the change was vital, taking this plunge would have been anathema to me.

I'm not talking here about courage that is brazen. Change agents don't display courage to let everyone know how bold they are. This kind of courage is displayed in support of the vision. The motivation behind my courage was to enlist the assistance of my boss in changing the organization's culture.

Having worked with lots of leaders, I was surprised at how open and non-defensive (and yes, courageous) my boss was as I broached this difficult topic. We agreed to a direction of change and I helped him write a memo to the conference employees and volunteers announcing it. The memo mentioned a change in the rules and expressed his support for giving more discretion to staff and volunteers in addressing issues previously governed by rules. The memo also assured them that there would be no second guessing.

It would have been one thing for the employees and volunteers to hear the news from me. It was quite another thing for them to hear it from the chief executive. To my delight, the memo had the desired effect. After the conference, it was reinforced with another memo celebrating the victories and mentioning none of the negatives.

Courage is change-making!

Survival Tip on Courage: *Do It Afraid*

Minister Joyce Meyer popularized (for me, anyway) the phrase, "Do it afraid." She makes the point that courage is not the absence of fear, but the decision to move forward even when we are afraid. In other words, we have confused feelings of fear with the lack of courage. Therefore, we disqualify ourselves from being courageous. Fear *will* come. Courage will act in spite of it. Without courage, we can take no action at all.

What helps me "do it afraid" is to avoid looking at whatever is causing me to fear. In the culture-change example I just shared, the thing that made me afraid was telling my boss that his actions were interfering with the change we sought. So I focused on the outcome of my "courageous act." I pictured people in the organization being more affirmed and validated; I saw a work environment made more enjoyable because the boss adjusted his conduct as a leader.

Focus not on uncertainty and the fear it causes. Focus on where the change will take the organization. And when fear comes calling, "do it afraid."

Sparking the Change

1. What chasm of uncertainty currently has your attention? What changes in perspective will help you cross the chasm in support of the vision?

2. What inconvenient truth are you wrestling with? Is the wrestling based in fear of what telling the truth might cost you? How is fear costing you the vision?

3. What single action have you been avoiding for fear of the repercussions? Make a plan to "do it afraid"; then evaluate the outcome. Was the step as

frightful as you imagined it would be? Was it as fruitful as you hoped?

CHAPTER FIFTEEN

SELF-PRESERVATION

While courage puts change agents in harm's way for the sake of advancing the initiative, self-preservation helps change agents know when to withdraw from danger. In this context, self-preservation is not about shrinking back from challenges to protect one's reputation or turf. It is about protecting one's health—physically, mentally, emotionally, and spiritually.

> "As personal commitment increases, so too must the ability to set boundaries and make healthy life choices."
>
> — Peter Senge, *The Dance of Change*

Great leaders know how important this is. The writer of the Gospel of Matthew recounts that after Jesus fed five thousand men plus their families, He went alone into a nearby mountain to pray. Jesus' famous relative, David, employed a similar practice in his day. He occasionally joined his brothers and King Saul, but also spent intervals at home:

The three oldest sons of Jesse had gone to follow Saul to the battle. The names of his three sons who went to the battle were Eliab the firstborn, next to him Abinadab, and the third Shammah. David was the youngest. And the three oldest followed Saul. But David occasionally went and returned from Saul to feed his father's sheep at Bethlehem (1 Samuel 17:13-15).

Change agents can get so caught up in shepherding the change that they burn themselves out. This is an unnecessary, self-inflicted wound. The problem may be that change agents and other leaders are accustomed to powering through their exhaustion. Physical exhaustion *can* sometimes be overcome. But it can also lead to mental and emotional exhaustion that can overcome the change agent.

For a very long time I worked at least ten hours a day at the office, came home to my family, had dinner, read the paper, and watched a little TV. Before going to bed, I would spend more time on my laptop. This happened five days a week.

On Saturdays, I also worked a few hours. And on Sunday nights, I worked some more. I was working so hard that I sometimes wondered why it was so hard to schedule Monday meetings. Until someone reminded me, I was too busy even to realize when Monday was a holiday.

Beware of Burnout

Becoming increasingly fatigued under this unhealthy regimen wasn't my only problem; I also became less like myself. I started treating anyone and everyone who did not actively support the change (including its intended beneficiaries), as enemies of the initiative. Exhaustion had shortened my fuse and dulled my perception.

Burnout can make any situation seem adversarial. It can also be fatal to change agents who fail to take care of themselves physically and ignore the signs of physical dysfunction. Granted, burnout rarely causes death, but it can have other negative effects, both physically and emotionally. These effects can be avoided *if* change agents are alert and responsive to the warning signs.

I happy to say, I'm still here; but during at least two major change efforts I helped lead, my stress level and blood pressure rose. Gradually I learned to watch the signs. When I became impatient, overly sensitive, less forgiving, or more critical, I knew I was headed toward burnout. Eventually, I also learned to schedule personal time by marking it on my calendar. I was run by my calendar. Anything not penciled in didn't exist.

It sounds almost pitiful to have to schedule something as obviously important as personal time, but I had to—and it worked. As time went on, I was able to get some rest, relaxation, and fun without scheduling it. I even gave myself a curfew—lights out on the work laptop by a set time each night.

It is hard to know what might have been had I not learned some self-preserving disciplines. Frankly, I'd rather not consider the possibilities. However, I am thankful for having learned my lesson.

Even change agents must learn to change!

Survival Tip for Change Agents: *Get a Life!*

During one of my change assignments, we would say good-bye to one another on Friday evenings by saying "Have a weekend." Having a good weekend was not top of mind; it was just "Have a weekend," *period.*

Change agents increase their chances of success and self-preservation by having weekends, making family a priority, and engaging in hobbies. That should go without saying, nevertheless...

Something helpful to my self-preservation efforts came almost by accident and definitely without any intentionality on my part. You might want to pursue it on purpose. It is called *friendship,* but it is friendship of a certain kind.

A friend has made it his personal mission to make sure I don't burn out. Seriously! He calls me from time to time so we can have lunch together. He lives close enough to my office that he sometimes drops in just to make sure I stop for lunch. He also shows up unannounced late in the afternoon to pull me away from my desk for a while.

These acts of friendship might seem like small things, but they make a huge difference and I appreciate them greatly!

Find someone who is willing to be a friend to you in this way. It will add tremendously to the quality of your life. You can ensure your future as a change agent *and* your self-preservation by getting and maintaining a healthy personal life.

Take the challenge...*please.*

Sparking the Change

1. Rate your self-preservation skills and your awareness of burnout. What do your findings reveal?

2. Are you watching for the warning signs of burnout? Have you seen them before? What choices did you make then; what choices will you make now?

3. At what point does your commitment to the cause of change become resistance to healthy changes in support of having a life? How does your approach to your schedule defy the change-readiness you espouse?

ENJOYING THE BENEFITS OF THE CHANGE

When the Philistines saw that their champion was dead, they turned and ran. Then the men of Israel and Judah gave a great shout of triumph and rushed after the Philistines, chasing them as far as Gath and Ekron (1 Samuel 17:51-52 NLT).

When the change Goliath is overcome, the organization can move forward and everyone can enjoy the benefits of the change.

I was proud to be part of several major change initiatives. Each one challenged me to understand the essentials of change, recognize the sources of friendly fire, and make good use of my arsenal of change "weapons." My hope is that the things I learned and have shared will encourage you in your journey of change.

Among the most challenging

most rewarding change initiativ

mentioned more than once: the trans

organizations into one. It was not chan

sake. *It never should be.* The streamlining

organization to implement cross-functiona

throughout its enterprise. These processes

supported the implementation of a new aut

system.

The transformation also created an environment

which cross-functional teams flourished. Cooperating

with other work groups became the default method of

working rather than a desperate means of avoiding

failure. Although the implementation was far from

flawless (large-scale implementations rarely are) it

was successful.

This success we enjoyed was reflected in the team

approach to solving problems and overcoming the

unanticipated obstacles encountered in any effort of

its size. The accomplishment was acknowledged

publicly when the company was chosen to receive an

international award for excellence in its field.

That's the good news. And there is more: the change agent survived to see it all come to pass!

May you and all change agents be similarly blessed.

REFERENCES

Side Bar References

Pg. 4 - Malcolm Gladwell, David and Goliath (New York: Little, Brown and Company, 2013), 6.

Pg. 10 - Hal Higdon, Marathon: The Ultimate Training Guide (New York: Rodale Books, 2011).

Pg. 19 - Mary Wollstonecraft Shelley, Frankenstein, or the Modern Prometheus (Hayes Barton Press, 1930), 158.

Pg. 24 - Robert F. Kennedy, "Address before the United States Congress of Mayors," May 25, 1964, the Department of Justice Library, http://www.justice.gov/ag/rfkspeeches/1964/05-25-1964.pdf (accessed August 15, 2014).

Pg. 37 - "Quotes on Change," Leading Thoughts, http://www.leadershipnow.com/changequotes.html (accessed August 18, 2014).

Pg. 49 - Peter Senge, *The Dance of Change* (New York: Doubleday, 1999), 9.

Pg. 57 - "Voltaire Quotes—Quotable Quote," Goodreads, http://www.goodreads.com/quotes/335536-one-day-everything-will-be-well-that-is-our-hope (accessed August 20, 2014). The primary source could not be verified, but the quote is fitting, nonetheless.

Pg. 66 - David A. Nadler, *Champions of Change* (Jossey-Bass, 1997)

Pg. 74 - "Bob Dylan Quotes," Goodreads, http://www.goodreads.com/quotes/11836-sometimes-it-s-not-enough-to-know-what-things-mean-sometimes (accessed August 23, 2014).

Pg. 87 - John P. Kotter, *Leading Change* (Harvard Business School Press, 1996), 115.

Pg. 94 - Daryl R. Connor, *Managing at the Speed of Change* (New York: Random House, 1993), 161.

Pg. 100 - Daryl R. Connor, *Managing at the Speed of Change* (New York: Random House, 1993), 147.

Pg. 106 - "Quotes about Tenacity," Goodreads, http://www.goodreads.com/quotes/tag/tenacity (accessed August 25, 2014).

Pg. 113 - Mary Anne Radmacher, *Courage Doesn't Always Roar* (New York: Conari Press, 2009).

Pg. 121 - Peter Senge, *The Dance of Change* (New York: Doubleday, 1999), 48.

Boxed Text References

Pg. 52 - Exodus 3:8.

Pg. 80 - James M. Kouzes and Barry Z. Posner, *The Leadership Challenge, Fifth Edition* (San Francisco: Jossey-Bass, 2012), 269.

Pg. 90 - Kotter, *Leading Change,* 130.

Pg. 97 - Daryl R. Connor, *Leading at the Edge of Chaos: How to Create the Nimble Organization* (New York: John Wiley & Sons, 1998), 56.

Pg. 103 - Richard Bevan, *Change Making: Tactics and Resources for Managing Organizational Change* (Seattle: ChangeStart Press, 2011), 66.

ABOUT THE AUTHOR

Greg Wallace manages and leads change as the Chief Operating Officer for HRock Apostolic Center, a ministry in Southern California, anchored by HRock Church, a thriving revival center in Pasadena; Harvest International Ministry, a growing network of churches, ministries, and missions located in more than sixty nations around the world; and the Wagner Leadership Institute, an international school of practical ministry.

A former executive at a Fortune 500 company, the author has successfully implemented change in a variety of contexts—in large organizations and in small groups, in corporate settings and in nonprofit environments, as a leader of leaders and as a colleague of leaders.

He has taught organizational change at Azusa Pacific University during his six-year stint as an adjunct professor in APU's graduate School of Business and Management. He has also lectured on organizational change at the California Institute for Advanced Management.

Greg holds a bachelor's degree from Cal State Northridge in political science, a law degree from UCLA, and a master's degree from Azusa Pacific University in Human and Organizational Development.

www.ingramcontent.com/pod-product-compliance
Lightning Source LLC
Chambersburg PA
CBHW060031210326
41520CB00009B/1084